IT'
INSURANCE BRACKET

THE PARTY: Your last opportunity to wear a lamp-shade and sing "Rock and Roll Never Forgets" into an empty beer bottle—and still have your friends the next day.

RELATIONSHIPS: You must decide how to spend the rest of your life—which means marriage for women and lying on the couch for men.

YOUR HEALTH: The bottom line—marry a gastroenterologist.

CAREERS: "Babysitter" and "busboy" just don't cut it anymore. Try aiming for "Neiman Fellow" or "manager of foreign bank."

APPEARANCE: No tattoos. No exceptions.

TURNING 30

ALEXIS MAGNER MILLER is a feature columnist for *The Providence Journal* where she writes a weekly piece on her favorite topic—herself. She is eminently qualified to write *Turning 30*, since she has turned 29 three times and turned 30 twice.

Alexis Magner Miller

TURNING

30

Hints, Hopes,
& Hysteria

Illustrations by Jerry Buckley

Ⓟ
A PLUME BOOK

PLUME
Published by the Penguin Group
Penguin Books USA Inc., 375 Hudson Street,
New York, New York 10014, U.S.A.
Penguin Books Ltd, 27 Wrights Lane, London W8 5TZ, England
Penguin Books Australia Ltd, Ringwood, Victoria, Australia
Penguin Books Canada Ltd, 10 Alcorn Avenue,
Toronto, Ontario, Canada M4V 3B2
Penguin Books (N.Z.) Ltd, 182–190 Wairau Road,
Auckland 10, New Zealand

Penguin Books Ltd, Registered Offices:
Harmondsworth, Middlesex, England

First published by Plume, an imprint of New American Library,
a division of Penguin Books USA Inc.

First Printing, July, 1992
10 9 8 7 6 5 4 3 2 1

 REGISTERED TRADEMARK—MARCA REGISTRADA

PRINTED IN THE UNITED STATES OF AMERICA

LIBRARY OF CONGRESS CATALOGING IN PUBLICATION DATA:
Miller, Alexis Magner.
    Turning 30 : hints, hopes & hysteria / Alexis Magner Miller.
        p.   cm.
    ISBN 0-452-26820-6
    1. Middle age—Humor. 2. Middle age—Psychological aspects.
I. Title. II. Title: Turning thirty.
PN6231.M47M55   1992
818'.5402—dc20   91-45604
                                                                      CIP

Printed in the United States of America
Set in Palatino
Designed by Eve L. Kirch

To G. Wing

CONTENTS

♦ ♦ ♦

INTRODUCTION

◆ ◆ ◆

Life is a series of milestones. Turning 5, for example, when you're afforded all the privileges and responsibilities of kindergarten, including head lice. Turning 13, when you develop an obnoxious personality and become anatomically correct. Turning 16, when you become legally entitled to drive a car through the garage door, and 21, when you're legally entitled to do it while intoxicated.

But nothing compares with turning 30, the point at which you must acknowledge—or at which others will happily acknowledge for you—the fact that time is catching up with you.

Make no mistake: It is. All through your 20s, you were in the bloom of youth. Bartenders would card you. Waiters would ignore you. Elderly women would pat your head and call you dear. You hated it. But trust me, in a few years you'll be willing to cut off your arm just to hear someone say, "I'm sorry, but I'll have to see some I.D."

30 is when you start worrying about all the sun you got in your 20s.

30 is when your metabolism slows but your appetite doesn't.

30 is when the kid who bags your groceries starts calling you "sir" or "ma'am."

30 is when you start getting junk mail.

30 is when it's all right to buy a washer. And a dryer. And life insurance.

30 is when it's no longer all right to ask your mother to do your laundry.

30 is when you're all grown up, whether you want to be or not.

Until 1994, when the last of the postwar generation will have hit this major milestone, people turning 30 will be called baby boomers. This is the most important generation in history—not because of its size or the influence it wields or the rampant consumerism that grips its members, but because it's the generation that invented microwave popcorn and perfected the art of lying on the couch all day.

According to actuarial tables, by age 30 your life probably is at least 40 percent over—and just think of how you've wasted it. At 30, Julio Iglesias had made love to half a million women. Vincent Van Gogh was well on his way to full-blown psychosis, and Roseanne (Barr) Arnold had reached her adult weight.

At 30, James Dean was a famous movie star, the idol of a generation.

And he'd been dead for six whole years.

Reaching—and passing—30 requires special strength.

This book may help.

Chapter One

THE PARTY

The most critical requirement of turning 30 is having a party, whether you want one or not. Some of us don't mind jumping the hurdle from young adulthood into approaching middle age and some of us do. But understand that your sentiments make no difference when it comes to the celebration of thirty-something status. Friends, family, and coworkers are all eager not only to acknowledge your birthday, but to broadcast it. Which makes one of my turning-30 coping mechanisms—namely, lying about my age—a bit difficult to execute.

Since a party is almost inevitable, try to see it in its proper light: as a rite of passage from youth to adulthood; as an opportunity to renew old friendships and reflect on your first three decades; as your last chance *ever* to wear a lampshade and sing a drunken rendition of "Rock and Roll Never Forgets" into an empty beer bottle—while still having your friends and family forgive you the next day. (Pull that stunt at 40, particularly around anyone from the office, and you may well find someone else behind your desk come Monday morning. At the very least you'll be a social outcast for the rest of your life.)

While I remained quite restrained at my own 30th bash, it was, nonetheless, an uproariously good time. My husband threw a surprise party, which meant I left the (very messy) house in a comfortable old pair of pants fashioned from what looks like upholstery material, and returned to the same (very messy) house where sixty of my nearest and dearest friends assured me that of course I didn't look like a walking loveseat and that they hadn't even noticed the clothes all over the bathroom floor.

Maybe you, too, can have the same kind of fun.

The Surprise Party

As I learned firsthand, the advantage to surprise parties is that you don't have to worry about what you'll wear or what your hair looks like. (Did I mention that I hadn't bothered to do anything with my hair?)

The disadvantage is that you don't have to worry about what you'll wear or what your hair looks like. (Did I mention that I was wearing it in a ponytail, a style that makes me look like Melissa Gilbert on "Little House on the Prairie"?)

Be prepared for some variation of the following:

"C'mon," your spouse will say, "let's catch a movie."

"But I haven't showered and I don't feel like getting out of my sweatpants," you answer.

"It'll be dark," he says. "No one will see you."

The man lies like a rug. Half an hour later you're walking into the classiest restaurant in town looking like one of the cleaning crew. "SURPRISE!!!!" a horde of friends, acquaintances, and semistrangers (all of whom, by the way, look marvelous) shriek as you try to calculate the distance between you and the nearest rest room.

This goes according to a corollary of Murphy's Law that says that the number of unexpected and/or desirable guests you have is in inverse proportion to how good you look. For example, it's a rainy Saturday and, to lift your spirits, you're doing one of those "total beauty routines" out of a magazine—the ones where models exactly half your age are shown "firming and toning" buttocks that have been bioengineered in a genetics laboratory. Your hair is slicked back with olive oil and secured under aluminum foil, your face is covered with mashed avocado, your thighs are wrapped in cellophane. In other words, you look as if you're ready to settle into a roasting pan for the afternoon.

The doorbell rings; it's several dozen of your friends, the majority of whom are carrying 35 mm cameras or videocams, and half of whom have chipped in for the male stripper who is performing right now on your doorstep.

Or you've gotten yourself a bottle of Grecian Formula and applied the stuff, then put on a shower cap to keep it from dripping into your eyes. And you've decided that what the heck, you might as well try out that tummy slimmer ("Put It On, Fat's All Gone") you ordered for $19.95 on a late-night whim. Midway through this self-improvement binge, the guys from the office stop by for a birthday brew. And you're standing there looking like Tinkerbell on a bad day.

Someday something like this will happen to my husband if, in fact, there's a God in heaven and She has any sense of justice.

Throwing the Surprise Party

There are times, of course, when it's you who is honoring someone else turning 30.

Reasons to throw a surprise party:

- They threw one for you (in other words, revenge).
- You've never forgiven them for telling everyone at work about your cosmetic surgery.
- You never want to hear from them again, and this is easier than a long, protracted breakup.
- You're relocating to the other coast and you want to make sure they never forget you.

Where to Throw It

Since maximum embarrassment seems to be the goal of surprise parties, you should choose a crowded and/or popular spot, one where the birthday boy or girl is sure to look completely out of place in jeans and a T-shirt.

Try the hottest nightclub in town, the new restaurant that everyone's been raving about, the lobby of a theater on opening night.

In fact, while you can hold a surprise party anywhere, the one place I'd not recommend is your very own abode. There's a chance the honored guest will be so embarrassed that he or she drinks excessively and either does significant damage to your property or falls asleep in your bathtub.

The Photo Album

This is a necessary ingredient, not only to remind the 30-year-old of his or her mortality, but to show everyone that, indeed, the guest's best days are behind her.

GETTING THERE

THE BEST EXCUSES TO GET A LOVED ONE TO A SURPRISE PARTY

♦ *To your boyfriend/husband:* "I think you're right that we need to expand our sexual horizons and that I was really closed-minded when I called you a pervert for wanting to sleep with me and my best friend. Shall we drop by her place with a bottle of wine?"

♦ *To your girlfriend/wife:* "I was thinking that I really don't spend enough time showing you how much I love you. Why don't we walk along the beach at sunset, have a romantic dinner, then shop for some jeweled token of my affection?"

THE BEST EXCUSE TO GET A LOVED ONE TO A SURPRISE PARTY LOOKING GREAT

♦ "I don't want to blow the surprise, but you're getting a really big promotion and the company's throwing you a party."

THE BEST EXCUSE TO GET A LOVED ONE TO A SUR-
PRISE PARTY VERY QUICKLY

♦ Arrange to have a friend call you at a certain
time. When you answer the phone, shout: "Oh
my God, it's the hospital! Your mother's had a
heart attack!"

♦ ♦ ♦

The Planned Party

While knowing about your party in advance takes
away the fun of being caught in upholstery material,
you will, at least, have input into the guest list and
control over what you wear. You can make sure no
one invites the office's Est convert or the neighbor
who gives everyone details about how she's coping
with menopause.

I would have appreciated the chance to suggest
that my husband not include a particular coworker
and his aggressive, Tupperware-salesperson wife at
my party. One minute I was making small talk with
a total stranger (and commenting, as I recall, on the
palm-tree crudité she'd fashioned out of bell peppers
and carrots) and the next I was buried under a
mountain of catalogs and sample plasticware.

(Yes, she pressured me into hosting a party—
phone calls at 11 P.M. will eventually weaken anyone—and yes, I hit on friends to come and yes, we
played games wherein you try to rhyme your name

with a vegetable and win a plastic cheese grater for your efforts, but that's another story.)

The Desperation Party

It's everyone's nightmare: What if no one remembers it's your birthday? You can pretty much guard against this by dropping subtle hints some weeks before the event. For example: "Gee, I can't believe I'm turning 30 pretty soon. (Pause for response.) In ten days, as a matter of fact. (Pause again for response.) That's the 10th of March. (Pause for response, raise voice.) Less than two weeks away. . . ." You get the idea. It may seem a little calculating, but I figure the only thing worse than suffering through a surprise party (did I mention I was wearing a sweater with a hole in the armpit?) is not having any party at all.

Therefore, if a reasonable period of time—say, a month—has elapsed and those invitations to the movies have turned out to be, well, invitations to the movies, you must take matters into your own hands. In terms of Life's Greatest Disappointments, not having a 30th birthday party ranks right up there with not going to the prom, not making the football team, and not ever once being chosen for Red Rover without the gym teacher yelling "SOMEBODY PICK FRED FOR CHRISSAKES!!!"

Host a party of your own. You stand a chance of getting great gifts this way; your friends will feel guilty that they forgot all about your birthday and will spend way too much on a present to make it up to you.

The main thing in throwing your own party is to avoid looking pathetic: if you extend invitations by phone, don't sigh a lot and let your voice break. If you mail invitations, resist the temptation to draw little frowning faces on the balloons or miniature tears on the clown. Under no circumstance should you pencil "R.S.V.P. or I'll kill myself" at the bottom of the cards.

The point is to avoid anything that indicates you are less than happy about doing this whole thing yourself. You are not just happy, you are ECSTATIC.

You're GLAD, GLAD, GLAD no one gave you a party.

You're PLEASED AS PUNCH at the chance to do it yourself and get it right.

You're THRILLED to be taking control of every aspect of your life.

You're LYING through your teeth, but no one has to know that, right?

The Birthday Party from Hell

One of my friends, a bright, intelligent woman who happens not to be married, said she knew it was too good to be true. Her parents were holding a dinner party, a small elegant affair, in honor of her 30th birthday. It just so happened that one of the guests, the son of her father's golf partner, was new to the area. And eager to meet people. And single.

And, she found out during the torturous meal, a mortician. One so thrilled by his work that he gave her a detailed description of the embalming process, doing his best to illustrate the story with a carving knife and the rock Cornish game hen. (She swears she'll never be able to look at poultry again.)

My friend suffered through what's commonly known as The Birthday Party from Hell. This is the one your parents give for you, the one to which, if you're single, they will invite that lovely son/daughter of Aunt Tillie's hairdresser's brother's dentist who is so nice but has trouble meeting people. (He or she will show up in ankle-length polyester pants and start crying after drinking exactly two beers.)

At this family gathering, be prepared to explain:

- Why you're still not married.
- Why you're still married to that loser.
- Why you don't have a job.
- Why you don't have a better job.
- Why you don't have children.
- Why you don't have more children.
- Why you don't have children who behave.
- Why a grown man like you insists on wearing a ponytail.
- Why you always have to dress in such tight/short/cheap/sloppy/vulgar/weird clothes.

There are acceptable answers—"Because" comes to mind, or "I don't know"—and there are unacceptable answers:

- Why can't you mind your own damn business?
- How come you're always bitching at me?
- I'm not married because I'm having too much fun screwing around.
- Ted may not be great but it's not like Dad ever did anything with his life.
- I don't have a job because I don't want to break with family tradition.
- My kids may not be well-behaved, but at least they won't all be in therapy when they grow up.

Gifts

I've found that one rule generally holds true: The better off the friend, the better the gift. I received some lovely silk scarves, hand-thrown pottery, beautifully bound books, and nice bottles of wine from friends whose careers I sneered at a decade ago ("Work for a cold, impersonal, soulless major corporation? Never!") and who could now buy and sell me, my husband, our children, and the dog. There are, however, notable exceptions. I'm thinking of the defective travel umbrella (it had a habit of popping open at inappropriate and/or dangerous times: in the elevator at work, for example, or as I was doing seventy-five on the highway) I received from a friend who is an executive with an accessories manufacturer.

Defective umbrellas aside, you should know that

certain gifts are inappropriate to receive as 30th-birthday presents. You would do well to rid yourself of any friend—or disown any relative—who buys you, or who sends to your party:

- Belly dancers.
- Strippers.
- Balloon bouquets.
- Candygrams.
- Theme T-shirts, especially if the theme is sexual. For example: the words "Wanna Hump?" above a picture of a camel.
- Vibrators, inflatable dolls, whoopie cushions, rubber dog excrement, or any other gift that would be considered riotously funny by your average 10th-grader (you're 30 now; this stuff isn't supposed to make you laugh).
- Underwear from your mother.

In addition to gifts you should no longer be receiving at 30, there are those you should no longer give. For more advice on this, turn to the next chapter.

Chapter Two

RELATIONSHIPS

In our teens, relationships were pretty simple. For him, the only issue was whether she would or wouldn't; for her, what counted were the letters on his sweater. As we passed through our 20s, relationships changed. For him, what mattered was whether she was willing to assume full responsibility for birth control and to deal with the consequences of its failure; for her, the issue was whether or not he stood to make any significant money in his chosen profession.

As you pass 30, relationships become vastly more complicated. Commitment becomes the issue, marriage the bottom line. For women, that is; thirty-something men would be content to date for the next 15 years, then dump the faithful but aging girl-friend for an 18-year-old with roller blades and a double-digit IQ.

That's because men are programmed to avoid commitment and women are programmed to seek it.

Sexist, but true. If my own research, which involves paying inordinate attention to the love lives of my still-single friends, is to be believed, there isn't a woman on the far side of 30 who wouldn't trade her briefcase for a wedding band and there isn't a man on the far side of 30 who isn't running for cover.

This is thanks to a basic biological inequity: men can father children until the day they die (one would hope, however, that the two events remain separated by a considerable period of time), and women have a deadline imposed by nature. The oft-lamented but hard to ignore biological clock starts ringing and women go in search of anyone who is remotely amenable to commitment ("Yeah, I'd like to get married someday, but we've only been seeing one another for eight years. What's your rush?").

Not, mind you, that being legally wed takes all the pressure off. Trust me on this. If you're already married, children will become the issue (see Chapter Ten). Or money will (see Chapter Five). Or both. By 30, you begin to realize that love doesn't conquer all; only cold cash and credit cards do. For this reason, you'll be less than charmed with a partner who's:

♦ Waiting tables while (still) Writing the Great American Novel.

♦ Waiting tables while (still) Writing the Great American Screenplay.

♦ Writing Poetry, the subject of which is The Meaning of Life, The Cruel and Capricious Nature of Love, or Why Capitalism Sucks.

+ Parking cars while waiting to be "discovered."
+ Slinging burgers while plotting ways to make a million bucks without ambition, energy, intellect, rich parents, or a sympathetic venture capitalist.

You will become less and less tolerant of your partner's more repulsive qualities—wearing polyester, for example, or starting every other sentence with "So I says . . ."—the thinking being that by 30, he or she ought to have outgrown them or have the sense to hide them.

It's good that you've become more discriminating, because the older you get, the more you're judged by the company you keep. You do not want to drag someone whose idea of an icebreaker includes, "Did you hear the one about the German shepherd and the prostitute?" to the corporate banquet. You do not want to go to Cousin Priscilla's wedding with someone who'll knock back Scotch all day and try to strip to the Hokey Pokey. You do not want to go to your father's retirement party with someone whose occupation is "exotic dancer."

But how do you judge someone right off? How do you know that under those pinstripes lurks the soul of an Amway representative or that beneath the Chanel suit beats the heart of a real estate agent?

One good way to tell who is and isn't mate material is to pay attention to the way he spends his spare time. Hobbies afford an unguarded glimpse into someone's private space. Run, don't walk, away if the object of your affection enjoys:

♦ Collecting baseball cards. It doesn't matter how many rare cards he owns, how many statistics he can cite, or how much his entire collection is worth. Ask yourself: Is this something Bryant Gumble does in his spare time?

♦ Collecting beer cans. See above.

♦ Collecting hub caps.

♦ Collecting dolls.

♦ Collecting comic books (unless the collection includes a first edition of Superman, which, in mint condition, is valued at $47,000 and which can, in a pinch, be sold to pay off the Visa bill).

♦ Assembling and displaying model anythings.

♦ Playing computer games. Only megawonks or megamillionaires such as Microsoft founder Bill Gates (who is both) are allowed this hobby after age 30.

♦ Raising guinea pigs.

♦ Breeding tropical fish.

If, however, your dearly beloved indulges in any of the following, you would be wise to get him or her to sign on the dotted line. Now.

♦ Collecting American gold pieces.

♦ Collecting art. The real kind, not the stuff that's advertised as "sofa size" and sold out of banquet rooms at the local Holiday Inn.

♦ Collecting rare books.

- Collecting fine wines.
- Restoring old houses.
- Breeding race horses.
- Raising and/or showing purebred dogs.
- Collecting quarterly dividends from the family trust.

The Concept of Parity

Before 30, relationships simply happen. Sex is the great equalizer, the glue that holds things together. That's why you will find a 21-year-old heiress dating a 21-year-old unemployed would-be musician who spends his days playing Nintendo and his nights playing bad rock 'n' roll.

After 30, all that changes. Parity is needed in every aspect of a relationship: wages, intelligence, looks, cars, apartments, domestic chores, and so forth. Things don't work when a post-30 Rhodes scholar dates a post-30 peabrain, no matter how attractive the package in which that weensy intellect resides.

But while parity has always been vital for post-30 relationships, times have changed. Parity today is different from what 30-year-olds saw growing up. Back then, according to household parity, the man's jobs were:

- Mow the lawn.
- Drink beer.

While the woman's jobs were:

◆ Buy the beer.
◆ Chill the beer.
◆ Serve the beer.
◆ Ask if the beer is cold enough.
◆ Wash the beer mug.
◆ Put the mower away.
◆ Do the laundry.
◆ Raise the children.
◆ Prepare the meals.
◆ Do the shopping.
◆ Clean the house.
◆ Care for the pets.
◆ Go to the doctor for a freely dispensed Valium prescription.
◆ Develop a serious addiction.

Today, parity means dividing every task equally—including such seemingly impossible ones as breast-feeding your newborn and worrying about prostate cancer.

You should know, however, that there's a critical point beyond which you will throw all concepts of parity right out the window, along with all standards. This may be when your youngest sister gets married and you spend the entire reception fielding questions like, "So what's wrong with you that you can't find somebody?" Or it may be right after your best friend has her third baby. Or when your boss starts making remarks about how some people just can't seem to settle down.

At that point, you'd marry your dog if the law allowed it. Instead, you settle for either the person you're presently dating (someone you wouldn't have looked at twice a decade ago) or the very next person who asks you out (also someone you wouldn't have looked at twice a decade ago).

Standards are reduced to: Is this person breathing?

Parity is reduced to each of you having a single nose and the same number of limbs.

Other Relationships

It's not only your relationship with your significant other that should concern you now. There are parents, siblings, aunts, uncles, and friends to be considered. If you are still relating to them as you did in high school (greeting friends with noogies and headlocks, for example, or giving your kid brother wedgies), it's time to grow up.

After 30, you are required to attend family gatherings; you may not blow town the day before your grandparents' sixtieth anniversary or pull a no-show at your brother's wedding. At all of these gatherings, you must be reasonably sober—or at least no drunker than your Uncle Joe. You must acknowledge important occasions—birthdays, anniversaries, christenings—with gifts (*real* gifts) and cards (*real* cards). You cannot weave your gift or build it in your basement workshop.

IOUs are not acceptable presents, and a do-it-yourself card is okay only if you're a professional artist or an 8-year-old.

GIFTS TO GIVE

PARENTS

Acceptable: A set of china, golf clubs, wine rack with ten bottles of good wine, tickets to a Broadway show, a Caribbean vacation.

Unacceptable: A note saying, "IOU One Anniversary Gift."

Relationships

SIBLINGS

Acceptable: Clothes, books, gift certificates to a decent restaurant.

Unacceptable: A six-pack of Rolling Rock, a used paperback, anything stamped "Irregular," a note saying, "Redeem for one night of free babysitting."

NIECES/NEPHEWS

Acceptable: Toys, books, clothes, savings bonds.

Unacceptable: A bag of candy, a coloring book, a kitten/puppy/baby chick/rabbit, a miniature drum set.

If you insist on giving cash, it must be in fifty- or one-hundred-dollar denominations, the point at which monetary gifts are considered generous rather than tacky.

Chapter Three

YOUR BODY, YOUR HEALTH

◆ ◆ ◆

Imagine the body you're born with as a supereffi-
cient factory. During the early years, thousands and
thousands of worker enzymes slave away for you,
tirelessly processing food into energy. Beginning in
your late 20s, some of these workers get lazy. They
start late and go home early. They take long lunch
breaks. Many of them spend the entire winter in
Florida. On the few occasions when they do work,
they convert calories to fat, a much easier process
than producing energy. By your 40s, these workers
have organized sitdowns and strikes, and by 70,
most of them have stopped working altogether.

While all of this treason is being committed in the
privacy of your own internal space, there are out-
ward clues, the first of which begin to appear in
your 30s.

Both Sexes

You will no longer be able to party all night and make it to work, bright-eyed and reasonably coherent, the next morning. You will no longer be able to make dinner out of sour cream and onion potato chips and a plastic vat of clam dip without paying a heavy price at 3 A.M., and you will no longer be able to eat Mexican or Chinese food without thinking you're dying three hours later.

In other words, you will have discovered heartburn, a condition that is easily relieved, provided proper diagnosis is made. Sadly, since heartburn closely mimics cardiac arrest, thousands of people—many still in their 30s—die each year, a half-consumed glass of Alka Seltzer in their hands. In determining the difference between heart attack and heartburn, the best advice is to marry a gastroenterologist: If one is not available in your area, a cardiologist or internist should suffice.

Males

One of the first signs of aging in men is the irresistible urge to join an amateur sports team, usually no-check hockey or twilight softball. Thirtyish men take their sports seriously. They buy uniforms, pose for team pictures, have stories in the newspaper, maintain standings and averages, and keep regular

appointments with chiropractors and orthopedic specialists.

The emergence of The Gut is another clear sign. Unless you are into bodybuilding (and no serious person after 30 should be), male bodies begin to slowly lose muscle tone. Finely defined deltoids and pecs begin to dissolve, and biceps refuse to bulge. Nowhere is the effect of aging more devastating than in the external oblique and transversus abdominis, which overlay the abdomen. Over a ten-year period, these muscles shrink until all that's left is fat—and not your everyday fat, either. This is adipose tissue that creates an actual metabolic craving for pizza and beer, instinctively consumed on a couch in front of a televised professional sports activity.

Having made such an investment in this portion of their anatomies, many 30ish men take perverse pride in their girth. Few, however, are pleased at other changes, namely those going on atop their heads. Thirtysomething men dread The Awful Things That Happen to Hair: thinning, receding, splitting, breaking, balding. Although many men enter their 30s with full heads of hair, few exit this momentous decade with hairlines intact, one notable exception being Ronald Reagan, whose success with follicles obviously came at the expense of nearby neurons.

So you must be prepared. Answer this simple question to assess your skill in coping with "mature" hair:

You've just turned 30. One morning, while in front of the mirror, three-quarters of your hair painlessly comes out in one giant tangle in your comb. Your first reaction is to:

- **a.** Calmly accepting your mortality, do your best with a new hairstyle.
- **b.** Make an emergency appointment with a dermatologist.
- **c.** Buy a hat.
- **d.** Buy a hairpiece
- **e.** Get drunk.

Answer: E.

There is no way to calmly accept mortality. Dermatologists have three-month waiting periods and they know as much about medicine as my dog. Hats are out of style, and hairpieces just don't work. Therefore, your best bet is alcohol.

Females

At 30, you will begin to understand why they make Control Top pantyhose and underwire bras. Namely, to keep things in place that used to stay there all by themselves.

You will begin to understand the rationale behind leg makeup and heavy foundation. Namely, to keep things hidden that used to stay hidden all by themselves.

You will begin to understand why they make bathrobes and one-piece bathing suits. Namely, to cover things you used to bare proudly.

You will become intimately acquainted with cellulite. Your thighs will ripple like sand at low tide, and your buttocks will look like the skin of a navel orange. In other words, your body, slowly but surely, will become your enemy. The comforting thing is that while you're losing the perfection of youth, you're gaining the grace and wisdom of age. Unfortunately, grace and wisdom don't count for beans in a bathing suit (which is why we vacation in Maine, where it's too cold to swim and where chamois shirts and chinos are considered a fashion statement).

Answer the following to see how well you'll cope with aging:

1. You reach down to smooth a bulge in your skirt, only to find that what you thought was your blouse is, in fact, your lower abdomen.
You:

a. Immediately join a health club.
b. Immediately go on a diet.

c. Change your clothes.
d. Go into the kitchen and eat an entire bag of M & Ms.

Answers: It's obvious—C and D.

2. You've put on five pounds and you hope nobody notices. But for the first time, when you ask your significant other if the extra weight shows, he says, "Well, maybe just a little."
You:

a. Kill him.
b. Kill him, then kill yourself.
c. Dig out his high school yearbook pictures and smirk.
d. Go into the kitchen and eat an entire bag of M & Ms.

Answer: D.

3. You're dining with your 18-year-old niece when the waiter asks if you and your daughter would like to look at the dessert menu.
You:

a. Kill him.
b. Kill him and then your niece.
c. Kill him, your niece, and the friend who suggested you come here for lunch.
d. Go home and eat an entire bag of M & Ms.

Answer: D.

4. One morning at work, while checking on your makeup in the company restroom, you notice a coarse dark hair growing out of your chin. You:

a. Scream.
b. Immediately pluck it.
c. Slip out to the corner drugstore, where you discreetly buy your first facial depilatory.
d. Leave work, go home, and eat an entire bag of M & Ms.

Answer: D.

With each passing decade women, like men, lose muscle tone, lung power, bone mass, and flexibility. However, women can compensate for aging. Unlike her male counterpart, the 30-year-old woman is entering her sexual prime, the time when orgasmic potential is greatest and least likely to be satisfied, given the fact that the average man's sexuality peaks at around age 12.

Why it happens. People assume aging is a biological process. And while biology is involved, so is physics: specifically, gravity. The same law of nature that brought an apple down on Newton's head inexorably pulls various body parts closer to the ground. By 30, for example, your spine begins to compress, the start of a process that will reduce your height by one percent a year until age 65, when you will be as tall as you were in sixth grade. Gravity also has an effect on the epidermis, that outer layer of skin that protects internal organs, helps maintain homeostasis, and, eventually, assumes the appearance of someone who's spent the last twenty-five centuries inside a pyramid.

What to do about it. There is nothing you can do about it, so you may as well accept it.

Wrong!

This is exactly the sort of pessimistic attitude that will mislead you into aging gracefully, which is positively un-American. In truth, there are many things that can be done to forestall aging. Consider Michael Jackson, who sleeps in a pure-oxygen chamber and continues, at 33, to act like a pampered, psychotic 14-year-old. Consider Madonna, whose 30ish breasts—with the help of appliances left over from the Spanish Inquisition—continue to defy gravity and laws of common sense and decency.

Those of you who are less ambitious can delay this whole slow slide if, on turning 30, you immediately begin A Program. A Program for 30-year-olds is not designed to make you look great or prepare you for athletic competition; it's designed to keep you from looking disgusting.

Programs can be established at home, but are best carried out at health clubs, where you can exercise on all sorts of modern equipment, then, after showering, consume a large meal and drink beer and wine while watching a wide-screen TV. The major drawback to any club is that one or two of your fellow members inevitably will be in respectable shape, despite having said goodbye to 30 a decade or more ago. These are the same sort of despicable people who drive BMWs and discuss soybean futures and South African Krugerrands in the sauna. God's purpose in putting such anatomical oddities on earth was to make everyone else feel bad.

If working out is too strenuous, men have another option. With practice, they can become quite adept at sucking in their stomachs; eventually it becomes a reflexive action, one triggered by walking past a mirror or within a quarter-mile of an attractive woman.

It is not physiologically possible for women to suck in their trouble spots—buttocks, thighs, hips— thus proving that God, who designed it all, is surely a man.

Another trick is careful dress (see Chapter Six, "Appearances Count"), provided you choose your wardrobe according to the same criteria the military uses—namely, for camouflage. This is why sweat suits have become the leisure uniform of baby boomers.

Cosmetic Considerations

First, wrinkles.

By now you have likely discovered, on close inspection before a well-lighted mirror, your first crow's feet. And by now you've probably developed a pretty good way of dealing with them: namely, denial. For some long time I convinced myself that the fine lines at the corners of my eyes were only there when I was tired. Or when I squinted. Or that you could only see them in bright sunlight.

So I did what every woman who's looking for assurance does: I asked my husband if he noticed them, and yelled at him when he, attempting to be both honest and tactful, said, "Well, maybe a little, if I look really hard."

These wrinkles-in-training provide a reliable predictor of what you'll look like at 50. This will enable you to plan your annual contributions to your personalized Plastic Surgery Fund, which you should open soon, considering that liposuction, tummy tucks, breast augmentation, and face lifts are not covered by most insurance companies.

GUIDE TO YOUR FUTURE FACE

Skin at 30	*What you can expect at 50*
No lines	Jane Fonda
Modest lines	Elizabeth Taylor
Crow's feet	Ted Turner
Slightly craggy	Charles Bronson

It helps, while moving though one's 30s, to have role models. By looking at how others have fared cosmetically, you can be inspired—or cautioned. Katharine Hepburn, classically beautiful half a century past 30, is a positive role model. Keith Richards, whose body has served as a living laboratory for pharmaceutical experimentation, is a negative one. (The only part of Richards's anatomy that may prove inspirational is his liver, which has survived the physiological equivalent of carpet-bombing.)

◆ ◆ ◆

Diet

In your teens and 20s, you took your health for granted. You knew you were immortal, and you consumed accordingly: Cheetos, Tab, cigarettes, and angel dust. If you counted anything that had to do with food, it was the price of a dinner out or, if you had a serious weight problem, calories.

Now there are so many numbers it can make your head swim: good cholesterol, bad cholesterol, overall cholesterol, LDL cholesterol, VLDL cholesterol, saturated fat, unsaturated fat, monounsaturated fat, polyunsaturated fat, beta carotene, soluble fiber, insoluble fiber, complex carbohydrates, and the combination to your home safe, where you've been forced to stash your M & Ms.

At 30, you will find yourself giving up foods you thought you'd eat forever. And in their place, you'll eat food you didn't even know existed. To wit, the dietary changes I've made as concessions to "maturity" ("a relatively new tendency to put on weight in unattractive places, which, if unchecked, will leave me looking like Roseanne Arnold"):

Before 30	*After 30*
Toast	Melba toast
Cheese	Cottage cheese
Coke	Diet Coke
Iceberg lettuce	Romaine lettuce
TV dinners	Lean Cuisine
Fritos	Unbuttered popcorn
Ice cream	Frozen yogurt
Sour cream	Plain yogurt
Hot fudge sundae	Apple
Frosted Flakes	Product 19
Pizza	Pizza
Beer	Beer

Dentistry

Before 30, dental hygiene consisted of regular checkups, an occasional filling, and, if your genes weren't quite up to snuff, orthodontics to straighten a few wayward teeth. After 30, things get serious. Teeth, like every other part of your anatomy, begin to fall apart.

Most 30-year-olds can look forward to gum surgery and root canals. Gum surgery is the less painful of the two, hurting only about as much as childbirth and taking only about as long. Fortunately, the procedure almost always entitles the victim to a prescription for Tylenol with codeine, a happy pharma-

ceutical which, if you ask me, isn't dispensed nearly freely enough.

Unlike gum surgery, which is usually a one-time visit, root canals are accomplished in several sessions. They include:

♦ The initial session, in which the dentist, a man who got his diploma at L'École du Marquis de Sade, removes the decayed root. If my experience is any indicator, a dull garden hoe is generally the instrument of choice.

♦ The second session, in which the dentist

makes an impression of your tooth with technology developed in the Inquisition.

♦ The third session, in which the crown should be put in place, but during which the dentist will find that the lab made a mistake and that the crown doesn't fit.

♦ The fourth session, in which another impression is made and another $200 is tacked onto your bill.

♦ The fifth session, in which the new crown is put into place.

♦ The sixth session, in which the dentist informs you that your dental insurance policy covers only the first $50 of the $2,500 cost.

I know of what I speak. I had my first (and only, so help me God) root canal recently. I went to the dentist for a routine checkup, and he—facing his son's college tuition bill, I suspect, or perhaps another payment on his sailboat—searched vigorously until he found a tooth so decayed it needed major (read: expensive) reconstruction.

"But it hasn't hurt at all," I said mildly, as he pointed to a vague, gray area on what he claimed was an x-ray of my tooth, but which looked like a map of Idaho.

"Not *yet* it hasn't," he said darkly. (It's not too tough to figure out who has the advantage here; one of us went to dental school and one of us has a morbid fear of pain.)

Which explains how I ended up in a chair with my head only a foot or so lower than my feet, mouthing incomprehensible responses to my dentist's attempts at idle chatter.

Dentist: So, how are the kids?
Me: Gnphggg, mnnn, lngnnnn.
Dentist: Mine, too. Did I tell you Junior's been accepted at Harvard?

Chapter Four

CAREERS

Okay, so I admit that I'm not wild about getting up at 6 A.M. every day and going to the office and listening to people who are, I'm convinced, not nearly as smart as I am tell me what to do. But I like my house. And I like new clothes. And my kids cost a lot more than anyone ever suggested they might (Have you priced soccer shoes lately? How about braces? How about a trip to the emergency room for the orthodontic equipment that, thanks to a soccer ball in the face, pierced an upper lip?)

And so I work. At this age, you should too. Look at it this way:

At 30, you are constitutionally qualified to be a U.S. senator. By 30, the pimply nerds you laughed at in eleventh grade are the doctors and lawyers who drive a new Mercedes every year. By 30, Queen Victoria had reigned for 12 years, Lindbergh had crossed the Atlantic, F. Scott Fitzgerald had written *The Great Gatsby*, and Steven Spielberg had directed eight of the ten top-grossing films of all time.

At the very least, *you* should have a job. It must be steady employment and offer health benefits, at least nine paid holidays, and, yes, even a 401(k). Unacceptable occupations for 30-year-olds:

♦ Free spirit
♦ Rebel without a cause
♦ Babysitter
♦ Paper carrier
♦ Car wash attendant
♦ Camp counselor
♦ Lifeguard
♦ Usher
♦ Peanut vendor
♦ Cheerleader
♦ Eagle Scout
♦ Male model
♦ Busboy
♦ Druggie
♦ Undergraduate
♦ Groupie
♦ Poet

Thirty is also a time when, sadly, you must put to rest many of the wonderful dreams of youth. For example, if you always longed to be a starting pitcher for the Dodgers and you're a bench player for the local Knights of Columbus softball team, it's time to wake up. Or if you always imagined yourself a prima ballerina but you're still struggling to shed those extra 30 pounds (and still inhaling Twinkies when no one's looking), you'd better give up.

Other dreams that don't come true after 30:

- ◆ Astronaut
- ◆ Concert pianist
- ◆ Rock star
- ◆ Miss America
- ◆ Professional quarterback
- ◆ Professional tennis player
- ◆ Model
- ◆ Heiress
- ◆ King
- ◆ Debutante

Graduate School

It's okay in a few professions to still be in school in your 30s. Medicine, for example, where residencies can last years and years. Law, provided you are a full-time student at a recognized university, not a night student at Degrees R Us or Sue U.

And there are certain rarified and purely academic pursuits—such as petrology, ancient Greek, or any branch of physics or biology that has the word "molecular" or "quantum" in the title—in which it is not only acceptable but required that you spend the best years of your life holed up in dingy stacks and dusty archives.

Otherwise, if you are in graduate school and in your 30s, you must ask yourself a tough question: What am I, nuts?

The answer is yes.

Living the student life at 30 is a grim prospect indeed. You will accumulate debt at a rate comparable to the U.S. Treasury. Your refrigerator will contain one moldy lemon, one head of decaying lettuce, a bottle of flat Perrier, two cartons of yogurt, a half-empty bottle of white wine, and a pint of Häagen-Dazs. You will not own a car, or the car you own will be a fifteen-year-old subcompact with a stripped first gear. You will do your clothes at a laundromat. You will ride a ten-speed bicycle wearing a funny-looking helmet and a rear-view mirror mounted on your scratched wire-rim eyeglasses. You will carry your things in a backpack.

But worst of all: YOU WILL STILL BE TAKING TESTS.

By age 30, the only exams you should be taking are those administered by qualified medical personnel (in which case it's up to them to come up with the answers). You should not be pulling all-nighters in order to pass a three-hour test on, say, The Introduction of Celtic Themes into English Literature.

Assume, therefore, that most graduate programs are ill-advised. In addition to having no food, no car, and no money as they pursue their advanced degrees, most grad students can—on graduation—look forward to having no job. This is because most graduate programs have absolutely no practical value. Ask yourself: What kind of career can you have after thirteen years of studying:

♦ Folklore?
♦ Comparative literature? (Does anyone really know what it is?)
♦ Medieval music?
♦ Sanskrit?
♦ Romance languages?

Note: None of this criticism applies if you've won a distinguished fellowship, if you're on sabbatical from a real job, or if you're independently wealthy and therefore can afford to do anything you damn well please, including stay in school for the rest of your life.

Self-Improvement

This isn't to say you can't do things to improve yourself. Remember, life is a great teacher and you should be its eager student, learning all the time. Which is why, after having done it once, you no longer slap your supervisor on the back and say, "How's it hangin', Hoss?"

There are plenty of places besides school where you can acquire the skills it takes to succeed. There's the library, where you can take out books with titles such as: *How to Make Several Million Dollars Even If You Have a Brain the Size of a Hummingbird's, How to Bilk Your Grandmother Out of Her Nest Egg, How to Marry Excessively Unattractive and Therefore Exceedingly Desperate Rich Girls, How to Breeze Through Life by Stepping on Little People.*

There are continuing education courses, usually offered at night at high schools and community colleges. You can learn accounting, business writing, data processing, or how to buy your next major appliance. Or you can take courses for fun, and learn ballroom dancing, macrame, or mixology. Since all these courses are taught by the same two instructors, neither of whom is certified to teach at an accredited institution, it's probably wise not to view "continuing education" as the ticket to your future.

You might want to consult in-flight catalogs, which advertise self-improvement tapes, books, and videos. Perhaps it's because these magazines hit a fairly upscale clientele, perhaps because they reach a truly captive audience. But whatever the reason, you can Learn to Be a No-Limit Person, Master the Neuropsychology of Self-Discipline, Succeed With Psycho-Cybernetics, and Have Unlimited Power for Peak Personal Achievement. You cannot, however, learn everything; you cannot, for example, listen to six audiotapes and take your neurosurgery boards.

Résumés

Before 30—when, basically, you've accomplished nothing except learning to tap a keg or go deeply into debt—you would put anything on your résumé to pad it. (If you didn't, it would have consisted of your name, address, and telephone number.) This was okay. Expected, even. Personnel departments everywhere smiled at your earnest, eager attempts.

The pre-30 résumé included:

- Moderate fluency in French
- Play piano
- Babysat younger sister four consecutive summers
- Class treasurer in junior high school
- Co-captain of JV softball team
- National Merit Semifinalist
- *Who's Who in American High Schools*
- Freelanced for monthy humane society newsletter
- Familiar with operation of 35mm flash camera
- Proficient at office machinery
- Drive standard-shift automobile
- Organizational skills

- ♦ Prom Committee
- ♦ Yearbook editor
- ♦ Merit badge in pigeon raising

Once you hit 30, nobody cares that you were a Lady-in-Waiting to the Prom Queen or that your SATs were over 1300. The only office you can brag about holding is one that's in a legitimate governing body (being treasurer of your bar's softball team doesn't count), and the only athletic achievement you can list is one you've accomplished on a major league team. In other words, you must have solid, grown-up achievements to put on your résumé.

What you (one hopes) can put down as a 30-year-old:

- ♦ Managed foreign branch of bank
- ♦ Had cash outflow of $1 million
- ♦ Oversaw department reorganization project
- ♦ Instrumental in passage of key health care legislation
- ♦ Pulitzer Prize finalist
- ♦ Neiman Fellow
- ♦ Nobel Prize in economics
- ♦ Generated sales of $5 million
- ♦ Never arrested for indecent exposure

Job Interviews

Here, as elsewhere in your professional life, you must act like an adult. When looking for a job, you may not employ any of the attention-getting techniques that worked a decade ago.

That means you may not parade back and forth in front of a major financial institution wearing a sandwich board that has your résumé on one side and HIRE ME—PLEASE! on the other. You may not stick your résumé under every windshield in the executive parking lot. You may not sneak into the company president's office with the cleaning crew, then shamelessly beg for a job.

Don't send a video of yourself singing "My Way" to the Personnel Department, and don't try to bribe your way through an interview with homemade chocolate chip cookies or the sweater you knitted for the CEO. The only bribery that works involves large sums of cash and/or the mention of your Uncle "Bobo."

You should know, though, that conducting yourself like an adult during job interviews doesn't mean being overly aggressive. Do not call your interviewer by his first name (and *absolutely* do not abbreviate his name, as in, "Charles, I'd really like this job. So, Chuck, pal, whaddya say?"). Do not tell your interviewer that where you want to be in ten years is sitting behind his desk. Do not slap anyone's back, slug anyone's arm, or ruffle anyone's hair.

You must dress appropriately for your interview. What was considered bad taste at 20 is, at 30, taken as appalling judgment.

For women, no:

- ◆ Cleavage
- ◆ See-through shirts
- ◆ Short skirts
- ◆ Seamed stockings

- ♦ Spike heels
- ♦ Teased hair
- ♦ Leather

You should wear exactly one pair of earrings, regardless of how many holes you've got in your ears, and you should avoid the purple eye shadow. If your babysitter says your outfit is "really rad," run back upstairs and change immediately.

For men, no:

- ♦ Chest hair
- ♦ Gold chains
- ♦ Tank tops
- ♦ Pinkie rings
- ♦ Motorcycle jackets

In other words, if Andrew Dice Clay could borrow your wardrobe, change immediately. Or apply for a job in New Jersey.

Chapter Five

MONEY
MATTERS

♦ ♦ ♦

Never forget: This is America, land of the free, home of Wall Street. Money matters; after 30, it may well be the sole criterion by which you're judged. In your 20s, it's okay to be a poor college student or a struggling young whatever. But by the time you hit 30, you'd better have a few bucks to your name (which I don't) or some clear idea of how you might earn them (which, since I only recently discarded network anchor, I'm still working on).

You should contemplate investing (if you, like me, are middle class, contemplate is all you will ever be able to do), perhaps buying stocks and bonds. You should also become fluent in the language of finance: Know, for example, that CD stands for something besides compact disc and that IRA isn't just an Irish terrorist organization.

You should buy life insurance, since seemingly healthy people do drop dead in their 30s for no apparent reason (not, of course, that *you* should worry about that pain you sometimes get in your chest or the way your left eyelid droops when you're tired).

The Budget

Unlike people in their 20s, who spend money without regard for tomorrow, 30-year-olds need budgets. My husband and I drew one up recently. We scrupulously recorded every single expense we incurred during a one-month period. We listed those expenses on one side of a legal-sized piece of paper and listed our income on the other. We added each column, noted that our expenses greatly exceeded our income, and applied for another credit card.

More Money

No matter what age, no one in America is ever satisfied with the amount of money he or she has. But unlike in your teens and 20s, when other priorities—namely hormones—got in the way, 30 is a perfect age to get serious about the task of accumulating more cash. One way, obviously, is to climb the career ladder. But that's hard work. And there are no guarantees.

I have a few other suggestions. One, which involves little effort and has the potential for a real payoff, is writing to the very rich, asking if perhaps they'd like to share the wealth. The direct approach is best here. You might try these:

Dear Mr. Trump:
   I know from reading your self-aggrandizing books and from following your divorce that you have more money than you need. So how about sending me some?

Dear Mrs. Marcos:
   Those pesky federal regulators! That whiny Corazon Aquino! How unfair that they're still nitpicking over the whys and wherefores of your accumulated wealth!
   I'd be happy to take some of the heat off you. Send whatever portion of the Philippine national treasury you'd like to my address, and I'll field all questions.

Dear Queen Elizabeth:
   I couldn't help but notice on your recent trip to the United States how big your yacht was. I think, frankly, it's too big for one family. May I (note the correctly phrased request for permission; the Queen is a stickler for—you'll pardon the pun—the King's English) move in?

Government Grants

   The federal government prints money and, with the right approach, will gladly print some for you. This is called receiving a grant.

Major organizations and serious artists and scientists apply for—and receive—grants every day. You can too. All you need is a good and/or obscure cause, and a form that's so full of difficult language no one will bother to read it.

While I can't share the details of my own quest for knowledge and federal dollars—we researchers are a closemouthed lot—I can suggest the following:

Tell the government you're doing research on a rare and endangered species. Make up a name (peruse the aisles of your local pharmacy; spell one of the products backwards) and a natural habitat. Your backyard will do nicely. Say your research involves how this creature adapts to modern life, specifically to the installation of an in-ground pool and tennis court.

Or say that you're doing research on cold fusion (all you need is a tumbler and tap water) and that you've been heating your house with the energy you've generated so far. If the federal government refuses to send you money, try writing to the state of Utah, and then to its state university.

If you can't get money out of the government, try keeping money from the IRS. Declare yourself a church, a nonprofit organization, a political party. (If you choose the last option, don't worry about having to run for—let alone win—any office. Take your cue from the Democrats, whose last successful election bid was so long ago that no one remembers it.)

One look at the finances of Jim and Tammy Faye Bakker should convince you that your best bet here is starting your own religion. Call it The Church of the Self-Involved. If asked for proof of its existence by investigators, say that your worship is very private and must be conducted within the confines of one's own home.

Be an Entrepreneur

If you're the impatient sort who doesn't want to wait to get money from rich people, or the patriotic sort who doesn't want to tap the federal reserve, why not make your own money? Start a business. A lack of ideas shouldn't stand in your way. Simply turn to the back of any issue of *Modern Romance* or *Soldier of Fortune* and find hundreds of ways to Invade Small Nations for Fun and Profit or Earn Extra $$$$$ by Licking Envelopes.

Be a Con Artist

Better yet, why not skip the working part and just print your own money?

Or come up with a plan to swindle gullible people out of theirs. Land deals involving far-flung tracts of Florida or Arizona real estate have real potential, particularly when pitched to the elderly. Ditto "investment" plans wherein people (again, the elderly are an excellent target group) give you their bank account numbers and you invest their life savings in a seaside villa in a country that has no extradition treaty with the U.S.

Inheritance

Or you could make money the old-fashioned way: You could inherit it. The fact that there's not a spare dime in your family shouldn't stop you. Just latch onto some helpless, rich old person and ingratiate yourself. Convince him that you are his child. If he refuses to believe you, tell him you're prepared to hold him hostage in Caribou, Maine, from December to March. Senior citizens are terrified of winter and will do almost anything—including moving to Florida or turning over the combination to the vault—to avoid it.

Dollars and Sense

The more you know about money, the better your chances of getting your hands on some. Test your fiscal IQ.

1. The business principle of laissez-faire means:

    a. Let the struggling, cash-poor little guy do it.

    b. Let the struggling, cash-poor little guy pay for it.

    c. Let the struggling, cash-poor little guy pay taxes on it.

    d. Toss the struggling, cash-poor little guy in the federal pen when he's three days late filing his 1040 short form.

Answer: All of the above.

2. Contemporary role models for the would-be millionaire:

a. Ferdinand and Imelda Marcos.
b. Ivan Boesky.
c. David Kennedy.
d. Danny Bonaduce.

Answer: None of the above. The principal value of having money is being able to enjoy it. Incarceration and/or death tend to make this difficult.

Business Smarts

The better your business judgment, the better you'll fare in the marketplace. Test yourself.

The following are sound investments. True or false:

1. Your cousin Joe, the only man to lose money in Southern California real estate in the late eighties, wants you to go in on a restaurant with him. He says since the idea was his, you're supposed to come up with the money. In cash.

2. Your neighbor's father-in-law is selling his earthworm farm franchise (Motto: All You Need Is Dirt) and declaring personal bankruptcy. You

see this as a golden opportunity to start your own business with a modest investment.

3. Your Aunt Dorothy got this hot tip about a sleeper stock that she says is going to shoot through the roof. It's a small company in Peoria that makes Super-8 movie cameras and electric typewriters.

Answers: All are true. For a booklet containing more proven money-making schemes, send $25, certified check only, to SCHEMES, c/o this book's publisher, Attn.: author.

◆ ◆ ◆

Cheap, Cheap

Regardless of how little money you actually have, it's important in the adult world you now inhabit to act as if there's no cash-flow problem. Don't hit your friends up for five bucks every time you see them. Don't stiff people over drinks or skate out without paying your fair share of the check. Don't always be the person who says, "Jeez, I'd love to, but I'm a little short right now."

In fact, regardless of your financial state, you should pick up the tab once in a while. (For how to afford this, see the Budget section at the beginning of this chapter.)

How to Spend It

Let's assume you've acquired some serious cash. Maybe you've won the lottery. Maybe the University of Utah gave you a big fat grant to generate power in a drinking glass.

Whatever the source, let's also assume you're not used to having this much money, and that you therefore have no idea how to spend it.

You should not, as a 30-year-old, act like some teenage lottery winner. You should not buy sports cars for all your friends, throw $5,000 parties, or go out to dinner and pick up the tab for the entire restaurant. You should not buy racehorses and powerboats and chalets in Gstaad. You should not blow $10,000 on a lost weekend with an aerobics instructor named Tiffany.

You should put something away, maybe invest in an earthworm farm.

Chapter Six

APPEARANCES COUNT

Without a doubt, the older you are, the more you are judged by the way you look. Shallow, you say? Unimportant, you insist? Get a life (and a shave, while you're at it), I respond. There are certain standards to which we, in our 30s, must conform.

I am not necessarily happy to forsake my chamois bathrobe for pantyhose and heels every morning, but I realize that the constraints of journalism demand I not dress from the nightwear section of the L. L. Bean catalogue.

You, too, should have the same sense of decorum. While standards vary from job to job, some basic rules apply:

Men. Unless you are a rock star, artist, or Native American, you must not wear your hair in a ponytail or braid. Unless you are an actor or a sailor, you would do well to remove that little earring from your earlobe. Regardless of who or what you are, take that ring off your pinkie. And under no circumstances—including being Don Johnson, whose popularity faded as fast as Miami's—should you have stubble on your chin.

Women. You must shave your legs. Ditto your underarms. You must find a hairstyle and pay someone generously to maintain it. The headbands and hair ribbons must go. You must wear makeup. And a bra. And perfume sold by the quarter-ounce, not the pint. Any clothes ever worn to a disco must be incinerated. Any shoes with heels higher than three inches must be given to your younger sister.

Both.
No tattoos.
No exceptions.

Just as turning 30 forced me to forsake Sara Lee for Lean Cuisine, it made me seriously reconsider my wardrobe. I recommend you do the same.

CHANGES IN ATTIRE TURNING 30 SHOULD BRING

***** WOMEN *****

Before 30	*After 30*
stirrup pants	sweatpants
bustier	bra
bikini	one-piece bathing suit
halter top	blouse
sarong	skirt
teddy	old sorority T-shirt

Underalls	Sheer Energy
Victoria's Secret	Talbots
Lycra	cotton
Spandex	cotton
Lurex	cotton
leather	cotton

Since the male fashion statement should, by 25, be confined to subtle varations in button-down shirt and rep tie, there's not much the thirtysomething man needs to alter in his wardrobe. However, there are a few basics:

***** **MEN** *****

Before 30	*After 30*
underwear	pajamas
underwear	bathrobe
jockey shorts	boxers

Skin Care

Because nature gave them different types of epidermis, facial needs of the sexes differ as people age.

Age	*Female Skin Care*	*Male Skin Care*
Teens	Good soap	Aqua Velva
Early 20s	Good soap, PABA-free sunscreen	Aqua Velva

Age	Female Skin Care	Male Skin Care
Late 20s	Good soap, PABA-free sunscreen, moisturizer	Aqua Velva
30s	Good soap, PABA-free sunscreen, moisturizer, foundation	Aqua Velva
40s	Good soap, PABA-free sunscreen, moisturizer, foundation, emolient	Aqua Velva
50s	Good soap, PABA-free sunscreen, moisturizer, foundation, emolient, collagen injections	Aqua Velva
60s and up	Good soap, PABA-free sunscreen, moisturizer, foundation, emolient, collagen injections, plastic surgery	Aqua Velva

◆ ◆ ◆

The Right Wear for The Right Place

Now that you're 30, you must give a nod to fashion. This doesn't mean being on the cutting edge of designer trends, wherein you show up at cocktail parties wearing a fake-fur-trimmed, bright-orange trapeze dress and matching chapeau (which looked ghastly on runway models and worse on you). It means, quite simply, wearing the appropriate thing on the appropriate occasion.

JOB INTERVIEW

> *Acceptable:* A suit.
> *Unacceptable:* Your college sweatshirt.

WEDDING

> *Acceptable:* A suit or dress.
> *Unacceptable:* A T-shirt and jeans.

CHRISTENING

> *Acceptable:* A suit, khaki pants, and a navy blazer, a dress.
> *Unacceptable:* Anything that shows any part of your body you wouldn't otherwise reveal in church.

COMPANY DINNER

> *Acceptable:* Conservative evening wear.

Unacceptable: Anything that shows any part of your body you wouldn't reveal at the office.

COMPANY PICNIC

Acceptable: Anything by L. L. Bean or Land's End; anything that looks like it could be by L. L. Bean or Land's End.
Unacceptable: Mesh tank tops, cutoff sweat- or T-shirts, hot pants, halter tops, Lycra shorts.

Shoes

It's important to note that after 30, shoes are an integral part of an outfit, not an afterthought. This means that you shouldn't be wearing sneakers with business suits (unless, of course, you live in a major metropolitan area and you want everyone to know how sporty and in shape you are, in which case you wear sneakers to and from the office—even if you only live across the street—and change once you get to work) or high heels with shorts. It means that your shoes should be polished, and your soles should be reasonably unworn.

Women should not wear superhigh heels anywhere anymore, and men should know the difference between Air Jordans and wingtips.

Also note that men must wear socks and women must wear hosiery on all business or formal occasions. It doesn't matter that you haven't worn socks since prep school or that you've got the best tan on the beach. You're an adult now, and, head to toe, you ought to look like one. Which leads us to:

Hair

For many 30-year-olds, hair is nearly as reliable an indicator of age as your birth certificate. By 30, men either start to lose it or worry about losing it. Sometime after 30, women become nearly as focused on what's starting to grow on their chin and upper lip as what's growing on their scalps. (See Chapter Three for more on this unfortunate subject.)

You will notice your first gray hairs and, if you're smart, you will pay someone (again, generously) to get rid of them. If you're not smart, you will try to do it yourself, at home, with something that promises to "wash away the gray." This is a little like trying to build your own porch without knowing anything about carpentry or trying to sew your own clothes when you can't thread a needle. You can spot an amateur's work a mile away, and trust me, the results aren't pretty.

Both men and women should make a concession to turning 30 in terms of the size, that is, height and length, of their hair. In other words, neither of you should sport tresses that cascade down your back and end in a trail of split ends somewhere around your waist.

Neither of you should have hair that, with the aid

of various gels and sprays, stands up and/or out more than an inch from your scalp, and neither of you should sport streaks of any color that looks like it belongs in a Crayola box.

◆ ◆ ◆

Actions Speak Louder than Three-Piece Suits

Appearance is more than the way you look. It's how you act. And post-30s should act like, well, grown-ups. In other words, they must have manners.

Dining Etiquette

Nowhere is this more important than when dining (the word 30-year-olds should substitute for "chowing down").

Know that it's not funny, and in fact quite rude, to belch loudly, then yell, "Well, excuuuuuuuuuse me" to everyone at the dinner table. Know that your days of drinking straight from the milk carton are over. Ditto the days of fingers in the olive jar. Know that the cardinal rule of mature eating is that once something is in your mouth, it must be swallowed; no spitting it back into your napkin or tucking it under your plate.

Telephone Etiquette

There are appropriate ways to answer the phone:

- "Smith residence, Jane speaking."
- "Good morning/afternoon/evening."
- And, of course, "Hello."

And inappropriate ways:

- "Yeah?"
- "Who is it?"
- "Whaddaya want?"
- "Joe's Bar & Grille, Joe speaking" (unless, of course, it *is* Joe's Bar & Grille and you are Joe).

Humor

Scatological humor is inappropriate for the mature man or woman. Flatulence, whoopie cushions, and bathroom humor are taboo. As are Helen Keller jokes, ethnic jokes, and jokes involving barnyard animals.

Other Guides to Good Behavior

No snapping gum.

No putting on makeup in public.

No questions about how much people make or how much they paid for something.

No gossiping in public—at least not when your target is within earshot.

No playing dumb (unless, of course, you really *are* dumb, in which case you can't help it).

Chapter Seven

HOME

RULE NUMBER ONE

You need one.

Because after 30, life is not a road trip and you are not one of its travelers. You must have a permanent address. You can no longer "crash" at a friend's "pad" while figuring out whether to join the Peace Corps or bike through Tibet.

RULE NUMBER TWO

By 30, your living quarters must be your own—yours and a loved one's, if such is in your life—not a place shared with eighteen other beer-swilling people, most of whom simply came to your last party and never left. (When they finally do go, odds are your stereo will go with them.)

THE REST OF THE RULES

♦ You must live in something larger than an office cubicle; it is no longer okay to cook dinner on a hot plate or unfold your bed every night. You should not have to rearrange the furniture every time more than two people stop by.

♦ You should own at least three pieces of furniture your parents would not criticize. Stereo equipment doesn't count in this category—in fact, you lose serious points as a grown-up if you're living with a $15,000 stereo system and still sleeping on a mattress on the floor.

♦ You should no longer be decorating with milk crates or lobster traps, and you should no longer think that lots of plants take the place of little furniture.

♦ Finally, you should not live like a slob anymore. Once a month, at least *look* under the couch.

Architecture

You never used to pay attention to what your dwelling looked like—at least not on the outside. Who cared what it was made of or what it was covered with or how old it was? You had priorities: low rent, laundry facilities, and a nearby bar.

You're 30 now. It's time to elevate your standards and broaden your horizons. In other words, you must start paying attention to where you live. You should know that a Federal house is not one owned by the government, that a Georgian isn't necessarily in a southern state, and that Colonial Revival has nothing to do with Puritan preachers and tents. You should know that a wing isn't found only on a bird and that a mudroom isn't someplace where nude female wrestlers work out.

Read books on the subject, take a course, rent a video, or join a local historical society. Better yet, hang around with pretentious people. They love to talk about the center-chimney Colonial they're restoring or the Queen Anne they're painting in period colors.

Which brings us to:

Fixing Your Home

Suburban thirtysomethings must either own a home or be in the market for one. Not just any house, mind you.

An old house. Old and run-down. Sure, you can often get a good deal on a place that looks as if the only thing holding it together is pigeon droppings, but money is beside the point.

Restoring an old house is the perfect 30ish pastime. That's because restoring an old house takes an inordinate investment of time and money. It is physically draining and emotionally exhausting. It gives you something to worry about, argue about, and talk about.

In other words, it's just like raising children. In fact, I think we've invested more in our house, which was built in the late 1800s and decorated by someone with aggressively bad taste (gingham wallpaper in the sitting room, sheet paneling nailed at an angle up the staircase wall) than in our daughters. Then again, we can't turn around and sell them for a profit, so I suppose there's some sense in this.

Major maintenance isn't confined to old houses. Newer-model homes never have enough space. The kitchen is the size of your parents' pantry and the bedroom is the size of a broom closet. Your only solution is to add on, which means you should block out the next 20 years of your life and 50 percent of your weekly pay until retirement.

This assumes you hire a contractor, a guy who will wear the same T-shirt and jeans every day for the several years it takes him to finish your two-room addition. The contractor will, for all intents and purposes, hold you hostage over the duration of your construction project. This is because he sort of knows what he's doing and you don't have a clue.

Regardless of how frustrated you become with his apparent incompetence and obvious indifference, always be nice to your contractor. Inquire about his health, fuss over the minimal progress he's made, ask about his wife and children. Offer him coffee every morning and beer by midafternoon, unless you want your windows put in upside down, the doors installed backwards, and the toilet to flush into the tub.

There is an alternative. You can spend twice as much money and three times as much time.

You can do it yourself.

Size

It is no longer okay to live like a Cub Scout at summer camp. If the ratio of people to bedrooms in your house is greater than three to one, move into a bigger house or kick somebody out (the latter is not an option with young children). However, if you live in Manhattan and the ratio of people to bedrooms is three to one, you should congratulate yourself. And maybe consider subletting some space as a source of extra income.

Furnishings

Your home should look as if you put some thought into it, not as if you acquired every item by yelling, "Wait! Don't throw that away!!!"

In other words, no Naugahyde recliners held together with duct tape. No kitchen chairs whose backs fall off when you lean against them. No springs poking from mattress or sofa.

Beyond that minimum, your home should give some hint that you know decorating applies to places as well as cakes. No AstroTurf carpet. No

lime-green sectional paired with orange plaid La-Z-Boy. No lime-green sectional, period.

Little Touches

You will hang curtains in the windows instead of relying on sheets, blankets, or dry cleaning that hasn't made it to the closet. You will occasionally use a tablecloth, and may go so far as to buy coasters. You will take all towels monogrammed "Hilton," "Sheraton," and "Holiday Inn" out of the bathroom and all glasses stamped "Leo's Lounge" out of the pantry.

Room by Room

Kitchen

At the very least, you should have food in the refrigerator ("food" means more than clam dip and a case of Bud) and plates on the shelves (they don't have to match, but at least four of them should be free of nicks, cracks, or chips). You should have a table and chairs.

Bathroom

CLEAN this room.

It is no longer okay to have a bathroom whose hygiene standards would offend Iraqi soldiers. No toothpaste cemented to the inside of the sink, no mildew on the shower curtain, no hairs plastered to the side of the tub.

Bedroom

Men: No posters of exotic sportscars, professional athletes, rock musicians, or large-breasted women.

Women: No posters of horses, ballet dancers, teddy bears, couples walking hand in hand through a field. No stuffed animals on the bed.

Both: No fake-fur bedspreads. No video cameras. No mirrors on the ceiling.

Living Room

You must have a couch—one that's decently uphol-
stered, not some yard-sale "treasure" covered with an
India-print bedspread—and at least one or two chairs
(beanbag chairs don't count and should, in fact, be
thrown out if you still have any left over from college).
Your television set should not be the largest piece of
furniture in the room.

No pictures of big-eyed children on the wall—unless they are your own. No paintings of JFK on the
wall—unless he was a family friend. No pictures of
Elvis anywhere, unless it's a recent photo taken in
Kalamazoo.

In General

Your house—or at least all surfaces in your
house—must be clean. After 30, no one will forgive
you for sticky floors and grimy walls. (You can wait
until 40 before you start worrying about the insides
of the refrigerator, cabinets, and closets.)

If you can't bear to clean your house, hire someone to do it. If you can't afford that, invite your
mother over for the weekend. She'll probably be so
disgusted by things that she'll go on a cleaning
frenzy in which she'll throw away everything of sus-
picious origin or indeterminate purpose (in other
words, almost everything you own).

Neighborhood

After 30, you must consider not only how you live and what you live in, but *where* you live.

In other words, you'll start to worry about The Neighborhood. For one thing, you'll want it quiet. This is true whether you live in Cowtown, Iowa, or midtown Manhattan. You will find yourself knocking on doors asking people to please turn down their stereos. You will call the police when a party goes until 2 A.M.

For another thing, you'll want your neighborhood to look nice. It will drive you crazy when people don't empty their trash or don't mow their lawns. The latter is because, if you are a thirtysomething suburbanite, you'll become aggressively involved in:

Lawn Care

Men: Your ego will become as inextricably tied up in your lawn as it is in your hairline. You'll do anything to maintain thick, healthy growth. You will invest money in fertilizers, super-duper mowers, weed wackers. You will be irritated if anyone puts a cigarette out on your front lawn and you'll be horrified if friends turn their cars around on the grass.

But lawn care is just part of the picture.

There's also gardening. For the first time in your 30 years, you will not only know what root rot is, you will worry about it. You will fuss over flowers and obsess over vegetables. You will actually hear yourself saying things like, "I'd love to, but I've got to go home and cover the tomatoes. We're supposed to get a frost." You may lose friends this way, but you'll have a hell of a salad to show for it.

Home Maintenance

Learn how to do it, or be able to afford to pay somebody who already knows. After 30, your home should not sport cardboard over broken windows or newspapers in lieu of insulation.

Take the following quiz to see whether you should fix something yourself or pull out the checkbook and run for the Yellow Pages.

1. Your faucet leaks. You:

   a. Ignore it.
   b. Make sure the drain still works, then ignore it.
   c. Call a plumber.

   Answer: None of the above. Ignoring it, whether or not the drain is unclogged, wastes water. Calling a plumber, *especially* if the drain is unclogged, wastes money. What you should do is put a bucket under the dripping faucet and water your plants each time it fills.

2. It's mid-January and the gas furnace goes on the blink. Suddenly your house smells like rotten eggs. You:
   a. Grab the air freshener.

b. Sit back, light up a cigarette, and decide how you'll approach this latest problem.

c. Run for your life.

Answer: The most important thing to remember when addressing minor household emergencies is not to panic. The correct answer, therefore, is B.

3. You're smack dab in the middle of watching Murphy Brown navigate her way through a blind date from Hell (and taking great comfort from the fact that even someone who looks like Candice Bergen can't find a decent mate) when the TV goes blank. And the lights go off. And the microwave stops radiating the Pop Secret. You:

a. Go down to the cellar and fumble around in the dark, looking for the fusebox.

b. Go down to the cellar with a flashlight and fumble around the fusebox, looking for some obvious way to correct the problem.

c. Go down to the cellar with a flashlight, uninsulated pliers, and a screwdriver and poke around the fusebox until the lights come on or you fall to the floor in a twitching heap.

Answer: C. It's not only the best way to solve the electrical problem, it's a handy way to revitalize your perm.

Plants and Pets

Every over-30 homeowner should have both plants and pets (certain low-IQ pets—golden retrievers, for example, or tropical fish—make plant-owning redundant) as additions to his or her life.

And just as the over-30's home should be maintained in a certain fashion, the over-30's plants and pets should reflect a certain level of care:

♦ *Plants.* No wilted leaves, no shriveled stems. Plants, contrary to what you may have thought in your 20s, need to be watered, not dried out in the oven and smoked.

♦ *Fish.* No more cloudy fish tank. No more letting the dead ones float on top until the other fish eat them. No more pouring beer in to see what it will do.

♦ *Dogs.* No mangy, underfed dogs. No fleabags. No more sprinkling marijuana on the dog's food to see if you can get him high.

Chapter Eight

GETTING
AROUND

◆ ◆ ◆

It's simple: You need a car. Even if you use a train or bus for the daily commute, all other transportation needs are best met with a car.

Your car should be reasonably clean, that is, empty beer bottles should not roll out from under the seats when you hit the brakes. The ashtray should not overflow. There should be no gum stuck to the dashboard, no dice hanging from the rearview mirror, and no Playboy air fresheners hanging anywhere. Empty paper coffee cups and old newspapers, however, are acceptable; this is grown-up trash.

UNACCEPTABLE CARS FOR THE MATURE DRIVER

◆ Yugo

You go and immediately trade this hunk of junk in for whatever you can get (somewhere between $50 and $100, provided the mileage is under 10,000).

♦ VW bug

Bugs are best known for their uphill performance: Passengers are required to get out and push.

♦ Camaro Z28

Z is for zipperhead, the best description of this car's typical driver. You are no longer in high school. Your friends are no longer impressed with what's under your hood. It is no longer appropriate to drag race down Main Street. Besides, a muscle car without muscle tone is a non sequitur.

♦ Van

At least not the kind with curtains in the windows and bumper stickers plastered across the back ("If this van's rockin' don't come knockin' "). The only van you should own after 30 is the one you bought because you, your spouse, the kids, their friends, the dog, and your returnable bottles can fit in it comfortably.

Acceptable Cars for the Mature Driver

♦ Jeep Cherokee
With four-wheel drive, of course—a feature you will never need, but will be able to brag about to your 30ish friends.

♦ Volvo
This sturdy, overpriced import is the perfect symbol of maturity, money, and deceit in advertising.

♦ Any pickup
Pickup trucks used to be the exclusive domain of rednecks. Then Madison Avenue stepped in.

Bumper Stickers

While almost any bumper sticker is in questionable taste, the following are simply out of the question:

♦ Shit Happens
♦ Fishermen have longer rods

- Nurses do it with patients
- Bowlers have big balls
- Divers do it deeper
- U Toucha My Truck I Breaka U Face
- I (Heart) My (Picture of Dog or Cat)
- Ex-Wife in Trunk

If you must advertise something on your bumper, make it a decent college or an environmental cause. If you went to an embarrassingly insignificant or inappropriately named institution—Beaver College and Ball State U. come to mind—buy a Harvard or Stanford sticker instead.

Also, by the time you hit 30, your graduation tassle should come off the rearview mirror. You should not have had baby booties hanging there in the first place, but if you did, those, too, must come down. If, after 30, you have one of those ceramic figures mounted in your rear window—the kind whose head is mounted on a little spring so it bobs annoyingly every time the car goes over anything larger than road kill—people have license to shoot you on sight.

Maintenance

Your car must be reasonably maintained. Coat hangers cannot be holding the exhaust system together. The trunk should not be tied down with hemp. Plastic should not cover a missing side window.

Men over 30 should appear knowledgeable about what's under the hood, even if they haven't the foggiest idea—and with today's high-tech engines, they usually don't. This means mastering the Diagnostic Ritual when the car breaks down. The Diagnostic Ritual begins when several men, getting wind of car trouble, flock to the disabled vehicle. With serious intent, they put up the hood, unscrew the air filter, check the oil, hold a flashlight next to something Electronic Looking, squeeze the radiator hoses, mutter something Mechanical Sounding to themselves, mutter something Mechanical Sounding to each other, pull a wire, crawl underneath, have someone sitting inside Try It Again, and finally go in search of a phone to call Triple A. The Diagnostic Ritual is most effective when performed for an audience of appreciative females.

Women over 30 should not be calling their fathers whenever the car breaks down. They should be able to handle auto breakdowns themselves. Which means they can forego the Diagnostic Ritual and proceed directly to the phone.

Getting Around

There are acceptable ways of getting around after 30, and there are unacceptable ways:

Roller Skates

Roller skates are out of the question, unless you're wearing them at your daughter's birthday/skating party.

Skateboards

Skateboards are absolutely taboo, either as a means of transportation (you need your head examined if you've ever even *thought* about this) or as a form of recreation.

Scooters

There are some things you're still too young for, and this is one of them. Riding these tiny, motorized vehicles automatically qualifies you for senior citizen discounts in Florida.

Bicycles

Bicycles are fine as recreation, but are only okay as a means of transportation if you're too young to have your license, if you're a graduate student in environmental planning, or if you are Angela Lansbury.

Walking

Walking as exercise is just right for thirtysomethings (see Chapter Nine, "Leisure"). As a regular means of transportation, walking is fine as long as you have a car. Meaning that it's okay to walk everywhere because you choose to, but pathetic to walk anywhere because you must.

Hitchhiking

People over 30 do not get rides by standing roadside with their thumbs in the air. This is because drivers assume, usually correctly, that over-30 hitchhikers are either escaped convicts or patients who slipped away from the State Hospital during this year's Annual Picnic and Field Day.

Automobile Etiquette

For the passenger, of course: If you are the driver, there is no such thing as auto etiquette, as anybody from L.A., Manhattan, or the entire state of Massachusetts will tell you.

Post-30 passenger etiquette demands that if someone gives you a ride somewhere, and that somewhere was at some distance, you must offer to pay for gas. Remember, this is not your high school buddy who's out with Dad's Gulf card. Your offer must be accompanied by bills or a credit card, not rolls of pennies or the change that's rattling around at the bottom of your purse. Passenger etiquette also dictates that you must offer to pay for parking (cash only and, again, no rolled coins).

And just as you must now sometimes offer to pay for things (for more on this, see Chapter Five, "Money Matters"), you must now sometimes offer to drive. Don't always be the one looking for a ride to the game, to the mall, to the party. Clean out your car *before* you pick your friends up; don't throw everything into the back as your passengers try to avoid sitting on Big Mac cartons and damp sweat socks.

♦ ♦ ♦

Subway and Bus Etiquette

On those occasions when you must forsake the car for public transportation, you should observe certain rules:

- ♦ Stand for the elderly and for pregnant women.
- ♦ Don't stick gum under the seats.
- ♦ Listen to a Walkman, not a boom box.
- ♦ Don't talk to yourself.
- ♦ Don't, under any circumstance, laugh to yourself.
- ♦ Censor your reading material. Save the copies of *Penthouse* and *Playboy* for your unseemly private moments.
- ♦ Censor your conversation. Don't supply your roommate with lurid details of last night's escapades while standing elbow-to-elbow with a carful of strangers.

Taxis

You must tip. Period.

Also, remember that while cabbies love to talk about weather, politics, and the hometown team, they are not your analyst. Therefore, do not subject them to the details of your latest anxiety attack, press them for a solution to that nasty business about your old boyfriend and your roommate's underwear, or ask them if they think the lump under your arm, the one you swear keeps moving around, might be cancer.

Air Travel

Air travel is the only occasion in life when you are forced to sit in a confined space for long periods of time in the company of perfect strangers—all the while wondering how many pieces you would be in if someone put several pounds of plastic explosive in the cargo hold. The true horror is that, unlike other stress-filled situations, you cannot turn to food for solace. "Airline food" is an oxymoron; one taste and you'll know why you never see cockroaches on airliners.

Nonetheless, air travel can occasionally be better than it sounds. Some lucky travelers have met the people of their dreams on airplanes. Others, through sheer coincidence, have made important business connections. One extremely lucky individual was able to win a multimillion-dollar settlement after his bridgework lodged in his esophagus during severe turbulence.

Alas, the standard airline trip doesn't have such a pleasant outcome. In one variation, a mean-spirited computer assigns you a window seat next to an overweight person with chronic halitosis whose greatest fear is flying, a fear that manifests itself in endless hyperactive conversation. In another variation, you will be confined next to someone who has just found Jesus and harbors the fervent desire that you find Him too, preferably before touchdown.

You must be prepared to defend yourself. Whereas the person under 30 might solve this problem by, say, constricting the offender's throat until his face turns blue, you—the mature 30-year-old—need to prepare a more subtle defense.

You should:

♦ Pretend to sleep.
♦ Pretend to read.
♦ Pretend you can't speak English.
♦ Pretend to have multiple personalities. (Four of them, including one strikingly similar to Ted Bundy's, should suffice.)

Chapter Nine

LEISURE

♦ ♦ ♦

30 is the first time you will choose staying in over going out. 30 is the first time you will choose eating in over eating out. 30 is the first time you will choose going to sleep over staying awake.

Vacations

Before 30, there really is no such thing as vacation—not in the grown-up sense of the word. There is spring break and summer fun and time abroad and time out and time off and time to find oneself, but there is not *vacation*, whose chief hallmark is matching luggage. Lots of it.

In the old days, you used to toss T-shirts and jeans into a backpack and take a charter (35-year-old aircraft with out-of-order restroom) flight to Europe where, with a copy of *Let's Go: Europe* and

$10 a day, you were happy as a clam. At 30, even the shortest vacation involves significant preparation and packing, which can last longer than your trip.

Consider the weekend on the Cape. In addition to ten pairs of pants, five jackets, six sweaters, four swimsuits, and a dozen pairs of shoes, your matching luggage should contain:

- Dramamine
- Dental floss
- Pepto-Bismol
- Your own pillow
- Vitamins

- ♦ Sewing kit
- ♦ First aid kit
- ♦ Blow dryer
- ♦ Curling iron
- ♦ Makeup mirror
- ♦ Tweezers, for those hairs that have started growing out of the mole on your chin.

Or consider our yearly trip to Maine. We take so much that we literally pack the bags around the children, then hope no one has to use the bathroom for the next seven hours.

Our first post-30 vacation was, in fact, to the aptly (but in my opinion inexplicably) named Vacation State. We exhibited unusual maturity for a relatively young couple, dispensing with many of the elaborate preparations and simply renting a house that came with everything we'd be leaving behind: two full bathrooms, a laundry room, and a microwave.

In choosing your hotel—yes, *hotel*—you now inquire into meals, bathroom facilities, wine list, room service, proximity to airport, cocktail lounge, air conditioning, and dinner menu.

A while ago my husband was headed south on a business trip (which is basically a minivacation at the company's expense). I heard him grilling the reservation desk about how late dinner was served, how early he could get breakfast brought to his room, and whether or not the facilities included a pool and sauna. This is a man who, in his significantly pre-30 life, used to visit me on weekends without so much as a toothbrush in his pocket.

While he's not shy about inquiring as to creature comforts, he does draw the line somewhere. He refused, recently, to ask whether the place where we were spending the weekend provided electric blankets and down pillows. So I packed my own. And his mother didn't seem to mind a bit.

Weeks before your departure, you begin paying attention to hijackings and terrorist alerts and are smart enough, as you pass through airport security, not to joke about the cordite bomb your traveling companion has cleverly built into his laptop computer.

Unlike the younger traveler, the 30-year-old must make elaborate arrangements before leaving town. Mail must be held, newspapers stopped, plants watered, grass mowed, lights turned on and off, pets fed and walked, neighbors notified, and credit card limits raised past your ability to ever repay.

Movies

No more watching movies that star Molly Ringwald or Bruce Lee. No more *Weekend at Bernie's*, *Police Academy* 1 through 25, or *Revenge of the Nerds*. It's time to tune in to sensitive, meaningful age- and sex-appropriate films such as *When Harry Met Sally* (women) and *Terminator 2* (men).

If your 15-year-old neighbor would watch it, or if they might be showing it at your old fraternity, you can assume this movie is too immature for you.

You can take a cue from its length: *Gandhi* is fine. Ditto *The Last Emperor*. And *Dances with Wolves*.

From its title: *The Unbearable Lightness of Being* is age-appropriate. As is *The Trip to Bountiful*. But not *Casual Sex* or *Hot to Trot*.

Or from its subject matter: You can see from the above suggestions that dramas exploring significant periods in history or significant passages through life are perfect viewing material, and that anything that focuses on the silly and/or seamy side of things is best left on the shelf (or rented when no one's looking).

Reading

Good-bye, Khalil Gibran. Good-bye, J. D. Salinger. So long, Kurt Vonnegut and Ken Kesey and Ayn Rand. Your tastes change after 30; you no longer owe a paper on every book you read.

Also, since your time and energy are now directed toward other, meaningful pursuits such as making money, dressing well, and trying to keep up with mortgage payments, you no longer have the energy it takes to plow through weighty (or even semiserious) tomes. There's no need to, anyway; you are no longer searching through literature for the meaning of life, having found it in the Hammacher-Schlemmer catalogue.

I still read—a good deal, as a matter of fact. But my reading material now reflects my (some would say quite pedestrian) taste as opposed to that of my English professors.

You might consider the following changes:

Before 30	After 30
Faulkner	King
Hemingway	Clancy
Dickinson	Steele
Salinger	King
Melville	Clancy
Alcott	Steele
Lawrence	King
Dickens	Clancy
Browning	Steele
Tennyson	King
Keats	Clancy
Joyce	Steele

It's not just novels that should reflect your newly mature status. Your magazines and newspapers, too, must be age-appropriate. This means that women should stop reading *Mademoiselle* and *Glamour*, men should put away *Penthouse*, and everybody should cancel the subscription to *Mad* magazine. It's time now for *Fortune*, *Harper's*, *Atlantic Monthly*, and *Barron's*. Unless your boredom threshold is at some perverse high, you will never read these, but it hardly matters. The point is to have them on your coffee table.

TV

The generation that grew up with "The Brady Bunch" knows good television when it sees it. Which is why, until network executives realized there's not much that's very interesting about watching a group of whining, self-indulgent people attempt to work through their angst every week, thirtysomethings had their own television show.

Relax. Even though our namesake series is gone, there are still plenty of shows for us to watch: "L.A. Law," "Cheers," "Seinfeld," "David Letterman," "Murphy Brown," "Designing Women." These are full of people who are just around our age—people who look a hundred times better than we ever will, people who are a hundred times funnier/smarter/ more insightful than we can ever hope to be, people who make a hundred times more in a week than we can expect to see in a lifetime.

Music

Many 30-year-olds cut their musical teeth on the Bee Gees, K.C. & the Sunshine Band, The Village People, and Donna Summer. But unlike the Bee Gees, K.C. & the Sunshine Band, The Village People, and Donna Summer, 30-year-olds survived the seventies. In the nineties, your musical tastes are mature. Included in your tape collection now are

U2, Don Henley, REM, and How to Improve Your Marketing Skills in One Easy Lesson. Another difference between your music now and then is where you listen to it. Instead of the ratty Radio Shack all-in-one combo stuck in your parents' attic, you tune in the eight-speaker graphic-equalizer stereo that came as a "special option" with your Toyota Cressida, for which you are in hock $18,500. Which is $12,000 more than you can afford. Which is why God created MasterCard.

Radio

You can tell your age by where the buttons on your Cressida graphic-equalizer stereo are set. Yours should include talk-radio and all-news stations. You are allowed two token FM stations, one that plays "album classics" and one that's run by college kids and calls itself The Cutting Edge or Rock Right Now. You will never listen to this station, but knowing it's there may help you feel young.

Sports

Unless you are a professional athlete, contact sports are out after 30. This is because your body begins to self-destruct (see Chapter Three, "Your

Body, Your Health"), needing no outside help at deteriorating.

But your athletic career needn't diminish with age. In fact, it can improve. Significantly. Even if you've never done anything more athletic than race up and down the aisles of the grocery store, 30 is the age when you can start to pretend you were once a superb athlete. Make up stories about high school touchdowns and field hockey championships. Refer vaguely to knee and/or rotator cuff injuries as a way of explaining why you no longer throw the old pigskin or jog ten miles at dawn. Comb yard sales and flea markets for old trophies and letter sweaters; store them up high enough so no one can read "Floyd Mertz, Skeet Shooting Champion, Class of '04."

Power-Walking

At 30, you do not jog, you power-walk. Power-walking, an ungainly pursuit made popular by ungainly presidential candidate Michael Dukakis, consists of walking with a very rapid stride, arms swinging to chest or even shoulder level, legs pumping, rear end poking gracelessly out behind you. Whereas jogging ruins your knees, compresses your spine, and jiggles every internal organ from adenoids to ovaries, the only danger of power-walking is a case of terminal embarrassment, since no creature, not even a duck, waddles this way.

Aerobics

You will opt for the low-impact, low-intensity version, unless your career goals include early retirement on SSI (in which case you might want to sweat and stretch yourself into lunch-hour frenzy, then collapse while climbing the stairs at work).

You will dress for class in a sweat suit or shorts and a T-shirt. You will not wear Spandex, Lycra, or anything so small and/or stretchy that it can be stuffed into your back pocket when class is over.

Swimming

You will still swim, but you will go about it differently.

Women: You will begin to look like a poolside version of your mother. Whether you've just had your hair permed and can't get it wet or you're wearing your contact lenses and don't want to lose them in the pool, you may opt for a sedate breaststroke rather than an aggressive crawl.

Men: You will now stop such life-threatening teens-and-20s antics as jumping off the garage roof and into the pool while covering your head with a beach towel or waterskiing with a beer in each hand and the line between your teeth. If your fear of paralysis doesn't stop you, the thought that you look just like a grown Beaver Cleaver ought to.

Thirtysomethings of either sex, unless they've regularly followed A Program (see Chapter Three), will perfect the drop-the-towel-that's-covering-your-cellulite-and-run-to-the-water technique. In this form of immersion, you shed your beach cover-up and tear into the surf in less time than it takes anyone to count the ripples in your thighs.

Other Manners of Sport

As with swimming, the way you approach many other sports will change. For example:

Cycling Not okay: Long distances at great speeds.
Okay: Short distances at your leisure.

Tennis Not okay: Playing with anyone who can recite, from memory, the top ten internationally ranked men's and women's players.
Okay: Playing with your grandmother.

Basketball Not okay: A pickup game with the guys at the gym.

Okay: One-on-one with your preschooler.

Baseball Not okay: On any team, however amateur, whose standings are regularly published in the newspaper.

Okay: At the company picnic.

Just as turning 30 signals that certain career doors are forever closed, your 30th birthday is the point beyond which you will not take up certain sports and leisure activities: weight lifting, for example, and gymnastics (the fact that the people who regularly win this event at the Olympics are 14 years old and weigh 85 pounds should tell you something). You will never dance with the American Ballet Theatre and, if you haven't done it yet, you will never, ever luge.

But take heart. Some sports, under any circumstances, are ideal for the 30-and-up set: croquet, bowling, golf, shuffleboard. The skills you hone now in these "sports" will serve you well right into old age.

Because sweat becomes less and less appealing the older you get, spectator sports are, in the long run, the thirtysomething's best bet. You should have a favorite baseball team, basketball team, and, unless you live in New England, football team, all of which you follow intensely. (Women: "follow intensely" means "should know which team plays which sport, and should have vague notion of said sport's scoring system," i.e., the Red Sox do not accumulate baskets, nor do the Lakers score touchdowns.)

Serious spectators read books, memorize statistics and box scores, collect memorabilia—which may, eventually, be worth something—and even come up with elaborate fantasies wherein they pretend to *own* certain teams. No kidding.

Chapter Ten

CHILDREN

Like a home, you need one. Or you should be at least thinking about having one. Or preparing a pretty good answer for your mate/parents/in-laws about why you don't want any.

These are plausible excuses:

- Gerald's facial tic may well be genetic.
- The world is a terrible, horrible place in which to raise a child.
- We've barely scratched the surface of our collective neurosis, and our therapist suggests we'd make less than ideal parents.
- We think Joan Crawford had the right idea.
- We're too worried about global warming.

And these are not:

- We just had that great, white wall-to-wall put in and kids would make an absolute mess of it.

- ♦ There's no room for a baby seat in the Alfa.
- ♦ Rover would have a terrible time adjusting.
- ♦ Gerald likes to think of himself as the baby.

The chief virtue of having children is not that they are your contribution to the human race. It's not that they'll afford you a kind of immortality. Rather, it's that your parents will focus on your children's faults instead of yours. Your parents will note that:

- ♦ They're undisciplined.
- ♦ They don't eat well.
- ♦ Their clothes aren't warm enough.
- ♦ Their hair is always in their eyes.
- ♦ They have dirt on their faces.
- ♦ They watch too much TV.
- ♦ They're always barefoot.
- ♦ They have no manners.
- ♦ They play too much Nintendo.

Having Children for Fun

Pregnancies may be planned or unplanned. Planned pregnancies happen when two people meet, marry, and realize one day they're getting killed on taxes. Unplanned pregnancies happen when people who can't remember to pick up their dry cleaning rely on anything but abstinence to keep from becoming parents.

As soon as pregnancy is reliably confirmed, you must tell the world. Do not—DO NOT—say that you are "preggers," a cloyingly cute expression that's completely inappropriate for mature parents-to-be. Use of that term is punishable by fine and/or imprisonment (where you will be forced to wear T-shirts that say BABY ON BOARD) in most states. Similarly, the Good Taste Police will arrest you for using such phrases as:

◆ Cake in the oven
◆ In a family way

- Knocked up
- In a delicate condition
- Eating for two

Note: No matter how in tune you two are, men should never say "we are pregnant." WE are not pregnant, SHE is pregnant. And WE should never forget that.

And Profit

Having a baby, like having a 30th birthday party, is a wonderful way to force your friends to buy things for you; you should seize this opportunity, since it is the only time your children will be a source of income.

There is, however, a price: a baby shower. Baby showers are festive affairs wherein mothers-to-be are expected to coo over the ten diaper bags, eight baby books, seven baby sweaters, five sleeper sets, and twenty-five baby blankets (all handmade by people who have apparently just learned to crochet) they're sure to get as presents.

One way to liven up a shower is to give everyone a graphic account of how the baby was conceived. After the narration, invite guests to share their own stories. Or pass out pieces of paper and see how many words everyone can make out of the letters in "pregnant."

Naming Them

Before 30, it's OK to give your children names such as Tiffany, Amber, Brandi (unless this is a twin whose brother is named Alexander), Stormi (unless your last name is Webber), or Aja. By 30, one hopes you have become a serious human being; the last thing you'd do is give your children names that people will laugh at. Thus you will not name them after colors, seasons, wildflowers, herbs, or foreign nations. *Indigo*, *summer*, *trillium*, *yarrow*, and *China* (no matter how you spell it) are *not* names.

Names should be found somewhere on the family tree—preferably right where one would find your oldest, richest living relative.

Dressing Them

It's definitely, infinitely cool—and shows very mature taste—to dress your children in itsy-bitsy designer clothes, or in anything by Benetton, Le Petit Bateau, Polly Flinders, or Laura Ashley. In other words, you want your children to be miniature versions of well-dressed adults.

What you DO NOT want is a miniature version of a grown-up punk: no little boys in headbands and leather jackets, no little girls in eye shadow and push-up bras.

Feathering the Nest

Once he or she is here, you'll need to find somewhere to put your baby. A guest or exercise room can be handily converted into a nursery; you lose nothing, seeing as how it will be years before you again summon the energy to entertain or exercise.

Standard nursery furnishings include a bassinet (a $2,000 piece of furniture which your baby will outgrow within six weeks), a crib, a changing table, a rocking chair, three mobiles, and eighty-five stuffed animals, none of which your baby will ever play with.

Preparing your home is perhaps the easiest part of expectant parenthood. Preparing your other children or—God forbid—your pets is a far dicier proposition.

A whole host of books has been written about easing children into the role of older sibling. Don't waste your money. All you need to know is that your older child will resent your younger child for the rest of his life. But bribery goes a long way toward smoothing things over; for the relatively low cost of a new swing set, you may buy a month's worth of peace. A pony costs more (and is inconvenient to stable in the city), but it's usually good for at least a year of calm.

Pets, however, cannot be bribed. Cats will resent anything small and cute that you bring into the house, unless it's small enough for them to "play with." Dogs are less susceptible to jealousy, but this is only because they haven't the neurological capability to master the emotion.

Discipline

Children need strong discipline if they are to grow into responsible adults. And you, as the parent, are the one to administer it.

Discipline has two forms: negative and positive reinforcement. An example of the former is when you tell a child who will not go to sleep that if he makes another sound, even something so quiet as a muffled sob, the wolf that lives beneath his bed will come roaring out and eat him up, leaving not so much as a fingernail behind. An example of positive reinforcement is when you tell a child who will not go to sleep that if he tries very hard, you will reward him in the morning with all the Fluffernutters, Reese's Pieces, Snickers bars, and Bazooka gum he wants.

◆ ◆ ◆

Communication

As any child psychologist will tell you, relating to your child is critical. By 30, many of us have pre-schoolers and even kids in grammar school. And many of us have engaged in some variation of the following conversation:

Parent: It's time for bed.
 Child: I have to use the bathroom.

Parent: (Escorts child to bathroom) Okay, now it's time for bed.

Child: I want a drink.

Parent: (Gets drink) Okay, now it's time for bed.

Child: But you didn't read me a story.

Parent: (Reads story) Okay, now it's time for bed.

Child: I have to use the bathroom again.

Parent: (Escorts child to bathroom) Okay, *now* it's time for bed.

Child: You didn't give me a kiss.

Parent: (Gives kiss) Okay, NOW it's time for bed.

Child: I need a hug.

Parent: (Gives hug) OKAY, NOW IT'S TIME FOR BED.

Child: How about another st—

Parent: That's not a *wolf* I hear, is it?

A FINAL NOTE

◆ ◆ ◆

You've read the book and presumably you're following all the advice.

You know what to eat and what to wear and how to spend your money. You know who to date and what to read and where to go on vacation. You know, in other words, how to pass gracefully through this trying decade.

That's right. With a credit card in one hand, a bottle of Scotch in the other, and a healthy—if aging—sense of humor.

Just to make sure you've got it all down, let's review a few of the mandates of turning thirty:

You must celebrate your birthday with a party. Whether you want one or not.

You must be involved in a relationship. Whether it's healthy or not.

You must at least think about having children. Whether you're ready or not.

You must have a real job and a real place to live.

You must own at least one suit.

You may not wear Spandex. Unless you're in a cycling event.

You may not mooch off friends (too often).

You may not draw smiley faces when dotting your "i's." Ever.

You must exercise. Or talk a lot about when you plan to start.

You must leave decent tips.

You must remove all beer cans from the floor of your car.

You must recognize that you are now an adult. Part of the grown-up world. A serious, responsible human being who would never even think of telling jokes involving farm animals and kitchen implements.

That doesn't mean you can't still have fun. Cut loose once in a while. Take a walk on the wild side. Hey, why do you think they invented duplicate bridge?

◆ ◆ ◆